TABLE OF CONTENTS

I0145806

WHAT DID YOU EXPECT?
IT'S A BOOK OF PUNS.

(IT GETS BETTER...)

LOCATION, LOCATION, LOCATION

FRUEDIAN SLIP $89.⁹⁹

WET-NAP

LIKE A SHORTER
WET DREAM

LADY THUG

ALIEN FOOD CHAIN

SNAPPING TURTLES;
THE JAZZIEST OF ANIMALS

NEVER JUDGE A TRIBUTE BAND
BY IT'S COVER... OH WAIT.

I ONLY MANAGED TO BUY ONE STAIR
AT HOME DEPOT BUT IT'S A STEP
UP FROM WHAT I USED TO HAVE.

THE HANDS ON MY CLOCK
CHANGE FROM TIME TO TIME.

OH YOU'RE A MUTE?
YA DON'T SAY!

IT'S A HARD KNOCK LIFE
AS A FRONT DOOR.

COLD AIR BALLOON

TRASH   RECYCLE   NICKELBACK CD'S

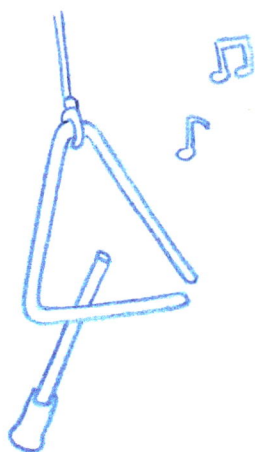

THE TRIANGLE

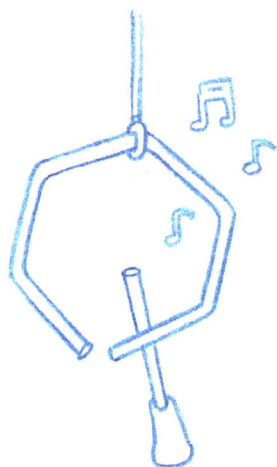

THE TRIANGLE
BY Gillette

now with
3 more
sides!

JASON BOURNE

JASON BOURNE 2

JASON BOURNE-AGAIN

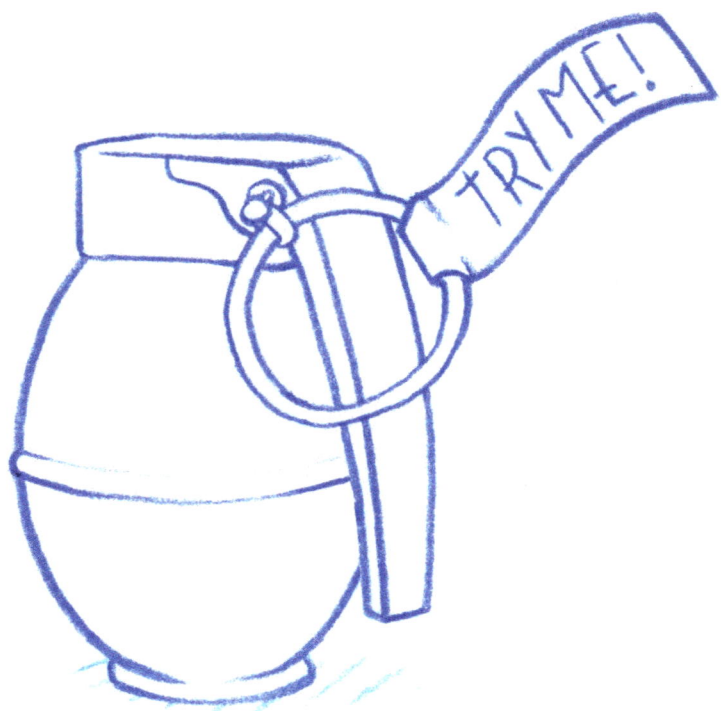

QUEEN O' FARTS

SOME CULINARY STYLES ARE DIFFICULT
BUT FUSION FOOD IS A PIZZA CAKE.

A BACHELOR OF SCIENCE IS B.S.

PSHT! A GRAVESTONE?
...OVER MY DEAD BODY!

THIS IS NOT NOT A DOUBLE NEGATIVE.

A SNAIL WITHOUT ITS SHELL
SHOULD BE FASTER BUT
REALLY IT'S QUITE SLUGGISH.

ME AND RECLINING CHAIR
GO WAY BACK.

OREGON
TREASURE
TRAIL

CLOWN SLIPPERS

BLINGRAY

ROCK   PAPER   SCISSORS

(NATURALLY)

HEADLESS HORSEMAN
HUNTING TROPHY

NEGATIVE SPACE SHIP

MON	9:00 - 5:00
TUE	9:00 - 5:00
WED	9:00 - 9:00
THU	9:00 - 7:00
FRI	9:00 - 5:00
SAT	11:00 - 0:00
SUN	11:00 - 2:00

A SIGN OF THE TIMES

SOME WORDS ARE INTERCHANGEABLE.
OTHERS, NOT SO POTATO.

MY TIME WITH LONG HAIR
WAS CUT SHORT.

MUST BE SO DRAINING, BEING A SINK.

I HAD A FEW IDEAS FOR
ALTERNATIVE SIDEWALK MATERIALS,
BUT NOTHING CONCRETE.

CROSSWALKS ARE SO PEDESTRIAN.

NOTHING MAKES ME JUST SNAP AT
SOMEONE IN A CLUB LIKE THEIR
SPOKEN WORD POETRY.

COCONAUT

GHOST SHIP

CAT NIP

NEW GUINEA PIG

TRAIN SMOKER

ANKYLOSAURUS
(cool)

ANKLE SORENESS
(not cool)

FINING NEMO

FRIAR HYDRANT

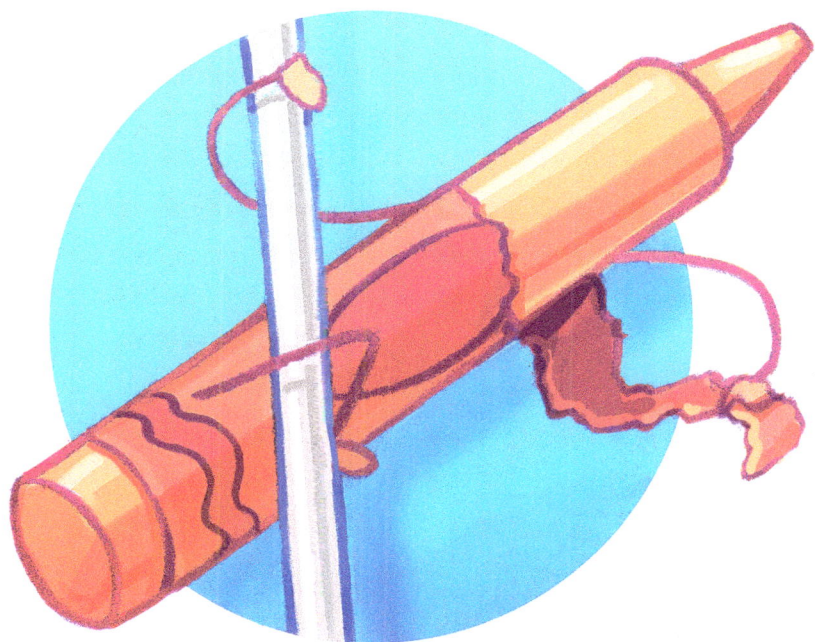

FIRE DISTINGUISHER

PITCHSPORK

A BAD CASE OF
THE STAIRS

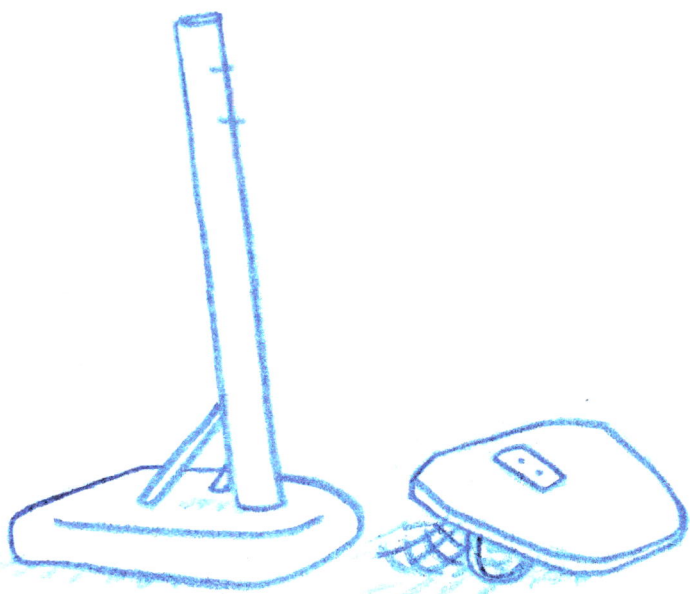

BASKETFALL

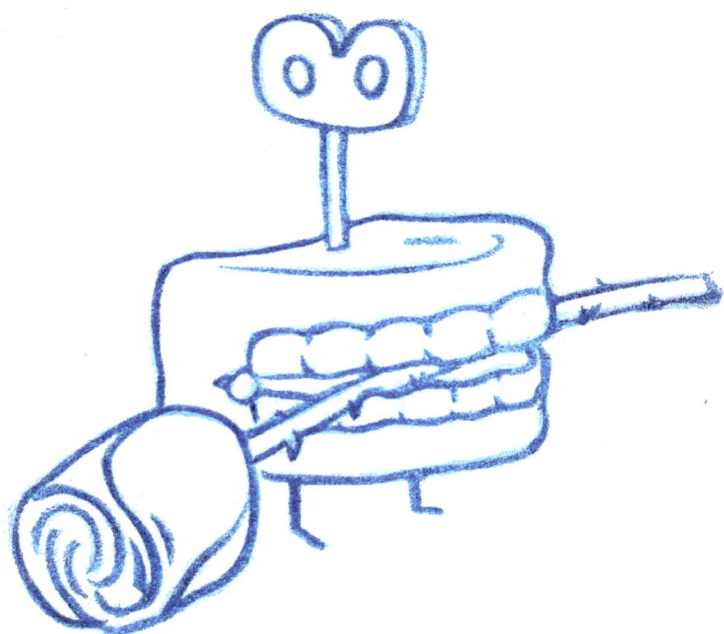

FALSE ROMANCE

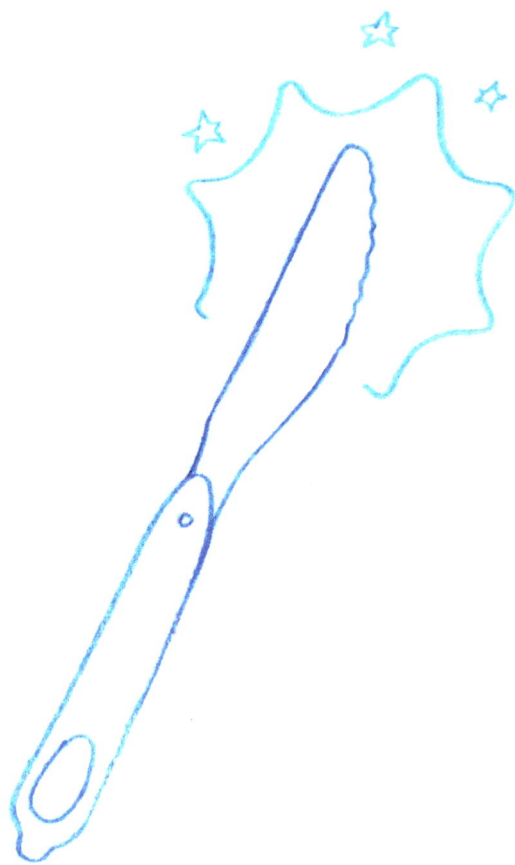

MAGIC WAND

(FOR CHEEZ WHIZARD)

KNIVES: CUTTING EDGE TECHNOLOGY.

THE PENIS ENLARGEMENT TRIAL
ENDED WITH A WELL-HUNG JURY

DISCOVERY CHANNEL COULDN'T HOLD IT IN...
THE ALL NEW =SHART WEEK=

"NOW, I DON'T HATE THE GUY...
BUT WISHES ARE A PRIVILEGE.
AND HE JUST KIND OF
RUBS ME THE WRONG WAY."

MEANIE IN A BOTTLE

RIP LINING

A LOUDSPEAKER

NOT ALLOWED SPEAKER

SUPER STOKER™

SHARPENER

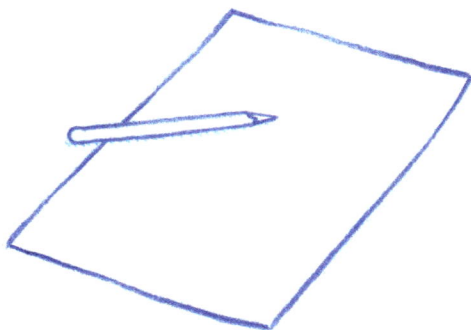

DULLENER

JACK-ALL IN THE BOX

JUNGLE JIM

FLOPPY
HAT

LAMP SHADEZ

HORSE-DRAWN CARRIAGE

FOWL BALL

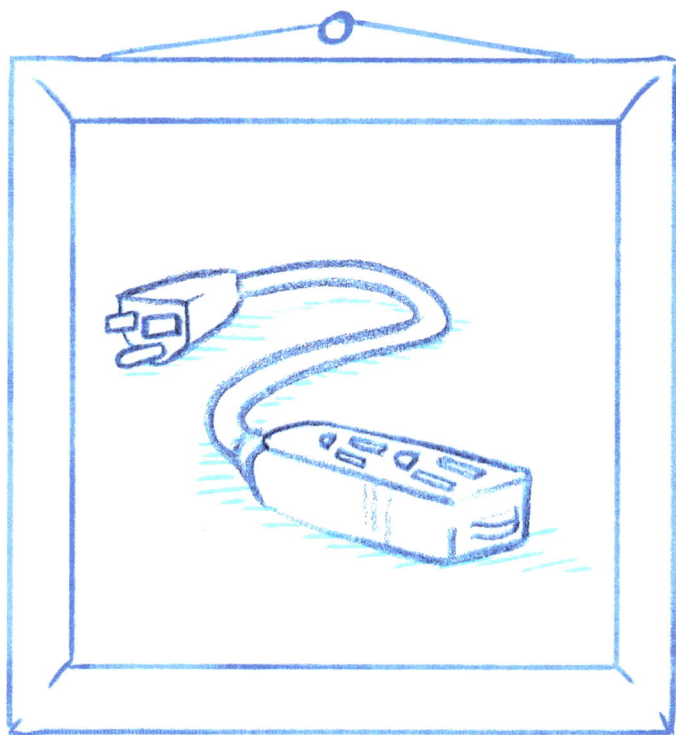

CORD EN BLEU

WALKING CANE

SUGAR CANE

HURRICANE

TONY HAWK

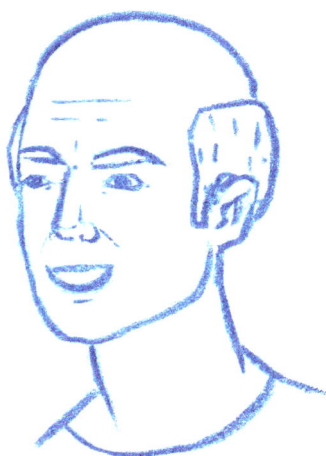

TONY BALD EAGLE

ASTRONAUTICAL

www.ingramcontent.com/pod-product-compliance
Lightning Source LLC
Chambersburg PA
CBHW041222030426
42336CB00024B/3416